MASTER THE ART OF RESUME AND COVER LETTER WRITING

A PRACTICAL GUIDE ON HOW TO WRITE A RESUME AND COVER LETTER THAT WORK LIKE MAGIC WITH PROVEN STRATEGIES THAT GUARANTEE EXCELLENT PERFORMANCE

DANIEL MORRIS

TABLE OF CONTENT

INTRODUCTION

There exists a ton of resources that offer resume writing "tips" and "tricks" but the fact remains that a lot of resumes out there are plain horrible. Some job seekers follow these "tips" to the letter without any positive result.

A job seeker once complained to me that after reading and following the suggestions he got somewhere, he wasn't able to get a single interview with the updated resume. Prior to following the directions he got, he was still able to get a couple of interviews with his old resume.

His plight informed my decision to create a manual that will provide concise guidelines, strategies and techniques for crafting a professional, quality resume that fits specific client career goals.

In this book, you will find a handy reference for crafting winning resume. Specifically what to do and what not to do when preparing a resume.

Whether you are a clerical worker who has not had the opportunity to help your business increase sales or a high achieving professional looking for a new job, you will learn how to write a resume that actually results to an interview in this book.

Have an enlightening journey!

CHAPTER 1

THE CHICKEN AND THE EGG: WHICH COMES FIRST

The conundrum has existed for ages - the chicken or the egg, which was here first. "Intellectuals" have argued the matter copiously in different directions. Some are convinced that the eggs were already here prior to the existence of chickens - the Dinosaurs created them, they claimed. Then there are others who would have none of those arguments. This set of people believes that the eggs could not have existed without chickens. "How could eggs exist when the creator of eggs was not yet in existence?" They queried. The answer to this question remains conclusively elusive. So the right answer to the question of whether the chickens or the eggs came first is "it depends".

Similarly, I have been in touch with job speakers who have asked the question "Does the cover letter or resume come first?"Others even ask whether they should write a cover letter at all. They erroneously assume that the cover letter serves basically the same function as the resume, hence it would be a waste of time to include a cover letter in their job applications. They couldn't have been more wrong. The job search process is dynamic and extremely competitive and it would be a dangerous mistake for you not to do everything possible to get that ever so elusive competitive edge.

SO, SHOULD YOU INCLUDE A COVER LETTER IN YOUR JOB APPLICATIONS?

Hell yeah! You should. You want to seize every available avenue to create an edge for yourself in your applications. The way to do that is to use every tool at your disposal. The cover letter is one of the tools that are indispensable when it comes to captivating recruiters and improving your chances of clinching that dream job. Not including a cover letter in your applications leaves you vulnerable to the deductive powers of the recruiter. The problem with that is the fact that these "powers" oscillates in tandem with the mood of the recruiter. It is dangerous to pin your fate on such an unpredictable rollercoaster and hope that Fortune smiles on you. You will only get the malicious grin of Failure bearing down on you as you struggle to rise from a stumble you took part in causing.

The cover letter is an avenue for you to create a unique aura of competence around yourself and significantly influence the conclusions and deductions of the recruiter in your favor. A cover letter gives you the chance to leave an unforgettable first impression on the recruiter and it would be a costly mistake not to write a cover letter for all your job applications. You would be shooting yourself in the foot if you fail to do so. So whenever you find yourself wondering whether you should write a cover letter or not, ask yourself this question:

Would I leave my destiny to the gnarly hands of the Fates or would I do everything I can to take my destiny into my own hands and shapen it for success?

Your answer to this question should direct your actions. And I trust you would answer it wisely. Now that we've established the importance of writing cover letters, it's time to address the 'chicken and eggs' problem.

COVER LETTER OR RESUME, WHICH SHOULD COME FIRST?

A lot of job seekers sending out applications find themselves unsure of the best way to submit their cover letters alongside their resumes. Hence, the reason most people completely omit the submission of cover letters altogether. Although Human Resource Managers have revealed that **they usually read cover letters first**, the only correct answer to the question of whether the cover letter or resume should come first in your submission is "IT DEPENDS". On what you might ask. The ideal way to submit your cover letter alongside your resume depends on the manner of submission of the application.

Before you decide on the appropriate way to include your cover letter for a job application, you must first determine whether the application is to be submitted electronically through an email, mailed to a specific address or submitted in person. You must also consider the modalities for submission cited by the organization. This will help you determine how to expertly include your cover letter in your submission to achieve maximum gain from it. I have documented the best practices for each method available. Adopt them whenever the need arises and you will never go wrong.

HOW TO SUBMIT A COVER LETTER AND RESUME THROUGH EMAIL

When you want to submit your cover letter and resume through email, it is very important that you consider the rules of submission given by the recruiter. If you fail to adhere strictly to these rules under the guise of being creative, it may cost you the job. If you cannot follow simple instructions, recruiters would feel as if you are too rebellious or simply dumb and you can say goodbye to the job. But when you are permitted to use your own discretion for the submissions, then there are three major ways for you to submit your credentials.

- **Submitting Your Credentials As a Single Attachment:** Submitting your credentials as a single document simply means you include a fresh page at the beginning of your resume. You will then use the fresh page to write your own unique cover letter, effectively turning your resume and cover letter into one single document. This document is then saved in the designated file format e.g. PDF, DOC, or DOCX. The only downside to this kind of submission is the fact that it might make it difficult for the recruiter to add your resume to their resume database if they have one. So you must proceed with caution when you use this method. This kind of document is submitted as an email attachment with a lean body in the email.

- **Submitting Your Credentials in the Form of One Document and One Attachment:**

Under this form of submission, you write your entire cover letter as the body of the email and attach your resume to the email message. This method is the ideal method of submitting your credentials to a recruiter. It guarantees that your cover letter would be read or at the least scanned if the recruiter is extremely busy. You must endeavor to use this method of submission as much as you are allowed to. The attached emailed would be subsequently downloaded by the recruiter after reading the cover letter. And it has the added advantage of providing an avenue for the recruiter to add your resume, independent of the cover letter, to their database.

- **Submitting Your Credentials As Multiple Attachments:**

Your submission can also be in the form of two attachments to the email message. One attachment contains the cover letter and the other presents your resume. You must take care that the two documents are submitted in similar file format. For instance, if you submit your cover letter as a PDF file; you must also submit your resume as a PDF file. Ditto if you use any other file format. In attaching your credentials to the email message, you must ensure that your cover letter is attached first before you attach your resume. It is also important that you clearly identify each attachment. The recommended naming format for the documents is as follows:

1. Ben_Shawn_CoverLetter.docx
2. Ben_Shawn_Resume.docx

Submitting your credentials in this form provides an excellent way for the recruiter to go through your documents and be able to keep a record of your resume in their database. The only downside is that it also makes it easy for recruiters to ignore your cover letter, unlike the previous format.

Of the three formats of submitting credentials, it is the second format that resonates deeply with recruiters and guarantees the actual perusal of your cover letter. Bear in mind that all of the above electronic methods of submission take the same email subject line in the format: Full Name_Position applied for. Example of an ideal email subject line for submitting your credentials is: Ben Shawn_Sales Manager. Practice these electronic submission etiquettes and you would have given yourself a remarkable edge over other job seekers.

HOW TO SUBMIT YOUR COVER LETTER AND EMAIL IN PERSON OR THROUGH POST

Although most companies would require you to submit your credentials through email or other electronic methods, there are still some companies holding on tightly to ancient habits of manual submission. These companies would either have you submit your credentials in person or have you mail your credentials to their office. In any case, they simply resent the idea of electronic submissions. It is necessary that you learn how to submit your cover letter and resume in the correct manner.

You must master the art of arranging your credentials in the most expedient and professional manner possible. The best arrangement is given as follows:

1. Cover Letter.
2. Resume
3. Portfolio of recommendation letter from your college or previous employers and other relevant documents.

The key to this arrangement is to make sure that your cover letter appears first, followed by your resume and then the others come in.

The Two Rules of Manual Submission of Credentials

1. Resist the temptation to fold your credentials. Never make the mistake of folding your credentials, any of it, with the hope of using a small envelope or folder. It communicates a negative first impression to the recruiter and it may even cause you to be instantaneously disqualified. Use a 9 by 12 inch envelope and let your credentials be straight and ruffle free.

2. Never staple your cover letter and resume together. In fact, you must never staple two distinct documents together. Remember: recruiters may want to include your resume in their database. Stapling your cover letter or any other document together with your resume is a minor inconvenience that could cause you a major loss. Avoid it. However, feel free to

staple the pages of your resume together if it is more than a single page. Alternatively, consider using a paper clip.

In this chapter, you have learnt the importance of cover letters, the best way to submit your credentials through electronic emails and the ideal method of submitting your credentials in person or through a post. It is necessary that you internalize the lessons in this chapter, master and expertly deploy them whenever you are submitting your credentials to create an unforgettable first impression on recruiters. And if you are ever in doubt as to whether you should include a cover letter in your job applications ask yourself this question:

Would I leave my destiny to the gnarly hands of the Fates or would I do everything I can to take my destiny into my own hands and shapen it for success?

CHAPTER 2

UNDERSTANDING THE DIFFERENCES BETWEEN A COVER LETTER AND A RESUME

Very few people understand the differences between a cover letter and a resume, This lack of clarity is also responsible for the confusion most job seekers face when it comes to including a cover letter in their applications. Since they believe that the cover letter is confusingly similar to the resume, they simply omit it in their job applications - a risky mistake.

Understanding the distinction between the cover letter and the resume will help you to develop a clear view of each of them and you will know how to craft each of them correctly and appropriately. Most importantly, you will be able to confidently jettison the notion that cover letters are insignificant and do not deserve to be included in your job applications.

The differences between a cover letter and a resume will be evaluated under the following succinct headings:

1. Length.
2. Level of detailedness.
3. Timeline covered.
4. Format.
5. Content.
6. Purpose.

LENGTH

You must understand the importance of the length of each of these documents. Realize that the length of each of them is expertly gauged to serve a different function and to serve that function appropriately, you must make sure your own documents conform to recommended specifications.

Human Resource experts recommend an ideal length of one page for all your cover letters. Submitting a cover letter that exceeds a single page is pushing the 'limits of nature' - of human nature. A lengthy cover letter could easily annoy a recruiter who still needs to go through a lot of other applicants' documents. So it is recommended that all cover letters must communicate powerful information in ONE page. On the other hand, your resume is expected to be between two to three pages long. A short resume made up of only one page communicates to the recruiter that you have not done enough for your career development and growth. It paints a negative picture of your professional qualifications. A recruiter may also be put off by an excessively long resume. Long resumes also have the downside of portraying you as an overqualified know-it-all that would be a nightmare to work with. You want to avoid this, so stick to the recommended length of two to three pages for your resumes.

By its very nature, a cover letter is expected to be shorter than a resume. That is the first and most basic difference between a cover letter and a resume. Always keep that in mind whenever you are submitting your credentials for a job application.

LEVEL OF DETAILEDNESS

Given the obvious disparity in the length of the pages of each document, it is expected that there wouldalso exist a disparity in how detailed they are. As you can guess, the resume is much more detailed compared to the cover letter. It is standard practice for you to refer recruiters to your resume for more information to keep your cover letter short. Never make the mistake of trying to match your cover letter to your resume in the depth of information contained. They are not in a competition, they are complementary. Realize that and allow yourself to submit a cover letter that is less detailed when compared to your resume. And never be afraid to refer a recruiter to your resume for more details.

TIMELINECOVERED

Another key difference between a cover letter and a resume manifests itself in the form of the timeline covered by each of them. While a resume is concerned with presenting a comprehensive account of previous jobs, education and accomplishments, the cover letter focuses on present and future career goals and objectives. This knowledge will help you to vividly discern the key significance of each of these two documents and it will also reveal why it is an act of extreme folly to seek to omit a cover letter from your job applications. Always keep this difference in mind whenever you are writing your cover letter. Know the different timeline covered by each of these documents and craft the contents in them accordingly.

FORMAT

You must also understand that the cover letter and the resume have a standard format that you must always structure your own documents after. Deviating from these standardized formats may cause you to lose sight of what is expected of you.

A cover letter is simply a formal letter professionally structured into paragraphs that flowand communicate effectively. The cover letter is structured like any formal letter; therefore it shows the recipient's address, your address, salutation, subject, body of the letter and the conclusion.

A resume, on the other hand, should be broken down into sections with bullet points that contain specific and relevant details like academic qualifications, jobs held and other accomplishments.

CONTENT

A cover letter is also different from a resume in the nature of the contents presented in them. A resume presents a comprehensive overview of your academic and professional qualifications and history. It lists all relevant skills and job experience related to the job you are currently applying for. Compared to this, a cover letter highlights specific areas of your career that is particularly relevant to the job you applied for and it also outlines how your current career goals align with the goals of the organization. In other words, while the contents of your resume may be industry-specific; the contents of your cover letter must be company-specific.

Succinctly put, a resume is often generic and formal whereas a cover letter is rather specific and more conversational permitting the use of relevant anecdotes to demonstrate your skills in action.

PURPOSE

The major difference between a resume and a cover letter is also clearly revealed in the purpose they each fulfill. The primary purpose of a resume is to provide a wide range of information concerning your education, skills and professional qualifications. It is the resume that makes it possible for the recruiter to gauge your skills and determine whether you are qualified for the job you applied for or not. The resume expedites this process by presenting relevant information in a format that makes it possible for the recruiter to determine your qualification for the job at a glance. A resume furnishes the recruiter with a record of your education, a summary of your qualifications, professional experience and memberships of any professional bodies relevant to the job you have applied for.

A cover letter on the other hand 'humanizes' all the data provided by the resume. It presents an individual rather than data. It communicates how you can actually use all your skills and qualifications to help the company achieve its own goals. It is also in the cover letter that you show that you are not all about the money by stating how helping the company achieve its goals also help you achieve yours.

Now that you have realized that some differences exist between a cover letter and a resume and developed a comprehensive and practical understanding of these differences, you will never make the mistake of underemphasizing the importance of any of them. They both fulfill specific functions that only they can correctly fulfill. You must realize that one does not replace the other despite all of their differences. Rather they masterfully complement each other. Make a mental note, and an actual note, of these differences and keep them handy whenever you decide to craft your cover letter and your resume.

CHAPTER 3

ELEMENTS AND FORMAT OF A COVER LETTER

Now that you have a clear understanding of the necessity of and differences between a cover letter and a resume, it is time to take a big step. In this chapter you will get to know all the elements of a perfect cover letter. You will learn what makes an amazing cover letter so amazing. Thereafter, you will have the tools you need to write a winning cover letter that captivates recruiters. But first, let's clarify what a cover letter really is.

WHAT IS A COVER LETTER?

A cover letter is simply a formal letter addressed to a recruiter which highlights your qualifications for a particular job and demonstrates convincingly how your skills and qualifications makes you a perfect match for the job.

I once took a course in marketing and the tutor emphasized the fact that most marketers make the mistake of outlining the amazing features of a product to a prospective clients in a bid to convince them to bring out their wallets or checkbooks and make a purchase or preferably several purchases. She concluded that statement by stating how "terrible and outdated" such marketing tactics are. Marketing is all about convincing people to do something most people dread - part with money. So telling a client that a house has three bathrooms downstairs, two upstairs, large windows and a basement will not convince him to buy it. You are making them do the work of determining how those features will be useful to them by stating all those features. Causing people to think too much during a sales pitch is a bad idea.

She went further to say that the only thing that potential buyers want to hear is 'how they benefit' from making a purchase at that moment. Rather than telling a client that a house has five bathrooms, tell him how he wouldn't have to wait to use the bathroom when he's already late for work. Rather than telling a client how big the windows of the house are, tell her how bright and ventilated it would make her home feel. Rather telling clients about the presence of a basement, let them know that they can use it as a storage room and create more living space. Or they can simply hide a body in there (just kidding!).

In other words features are bland, tedious facts that people find cumbersome to deal with. Benefits on the other hand make people excited and willing to take up whatever you offer. In the same vein, your resume presents a list of facts that cannot convince anyone to hire you no matter how impressive they are. It is your cover letter that demonstrates how those features will benefit your employer. It is your own personal sales pitch. It gives you the opportunity to let the recruiter know how you can use your skills and education -features- to deliver value for the organization -benefits.

With that clear and unmistakable picture of a cover letter in mind, we must now proceed to the elements of a cover letter. What makes a great cover letter different from just 'any' cover letter?

ELEMENTS OF A COVER LETTER EXPLAINED

Every cover letter has the following elements that make them a cover letter worthy of consideration:

1. Your name and address.
2. Date.
3. Recipient company details.
4. Salutation.
5. An introduction.
6. A carefully structured body.
7. Closing paragraph.
8. Complimentary close.
9. Postscript.

Your Name and Address

Every time you start a cover letter, your own name and address must appear first. Your full name as obtainable in your resume must be the first thing a recruiter sees on your cover letter. Then your contact details and correct address must follow. Some experts advocate including a link to your LinkedIn profile if you are submitting an electronic copy of your cover letter rather than mailing it to the company. Feel free to do this if you have a professional looking LinkedIn profile but NEVER make the mistake of including other social media links in your applications. No one is interested in your FaceBook or Instagram details, keep those to yourself.

There are several formats for presenting your name and address on a cover letter but it is ideal that you use a format that shows your address aligned to the left-hand side.

Date

Date is an indispensable element of every cover letter, never omit it. The date must show the date you are sending or submitting the cover letter. The date on a cover letter follows any of the following dating formats:

- June 25, 20x0
- 25 June, 20x0

Apply one of the above formats in your cover letter and make sure you avoid any of the following formats of writing dates or any of their variations:

- 22-06-20x0
- 22/06/20x0

Write your date correctly and format it appropriately. The date comes after your own address and before your recipient's address but you must take care to **leave a space after your own address and before the recipient's address**. It is very important that you do not cluster the addresses on your cover letter together. Leaving a space after your own address like you would after a paragraph before writing your date and after writing it will make your cover letter neat and presentable. Practice this in all the cover letters you write.

Recipient's Address

After the date, the recipient's address is the next element in a cover letter. You must learn to personalize the recipient's address by making sure you insert the full name of the hiring manager or the Human Resource Director at the top of the address. You can get this crucial detail from the company's website or through other websites that companies list their details. Ensure you find that name and use it to top your recipient's address. It communicates positively of you.

Salutation

Remember that a cover letter is still a letter, therefore it is important that you include the appropriate salutations. Here again, you will need to use the name of the hiring manager. It conveys a sense of cordiality that could be very useful to you. The acceptable formats of a salutation for cover letters include:

- Using a title and the last name of the recruiter. E.g. *Dear Mr. Washington.* A salutation like this is formal, yet personal.

- Using the first name of the recruiter. E.g. *Dear Kyle.* This is a somewhat less formal salutation but it sure grabs attention quickly.

- Use the job title of the recruiter. E.g. *Dear Hiring Manager.* This is the last resort when you have tried and failed to find the name of the recruiter. However do not use this as an excuse to be lazy. Ensure you carry out due diligence before you use such a format.

Select the appropriate salutation based on your own discretion. But bear in mind that some recruiters see the second format of salutation as too informal and familiar. So I'd recommend you stick to the first format of salutation.

There are certain formats of salutation that are simply off-putting and downright repulsive. You must learn to always avoid them at all cost. Never use the following form of salutation in your cover letter:

- *To whom it may concern.* This salutation is terrible. It comes off as excessively formal and portrays you as a stuck-up individual that could be a chore to work with. Avoid it at all costs. A salutation like this may also convey the fact that you are too lazy to conduct a directed and organized research needed to get the name of the recruiter.

- *Hey.* If you ever submit a cover letter with a salutation like this, you can forget about the job already. No recruiter will read a cover letter that starts like that. It is too casual and lackadaisical.

- *Hi.* You cannot use this salutation for the same reasons you cannot use '*Hey*'.

Your salutation is very vital in a cover letter. It sets the tone for the entire letter so endeavor to get it right.

An Introduction

The introduction is the first paragraph presented in your cover letter. It makes or mars the entire letter. Your introduction is what determines whether the recruiter will continue to read the cover letter or not. Hence, it must be very captivating. Find a way to incorporate the name of the company in the first paragraph of the cover letter. It shows that you are sending a letter specifically written for that organization and not a generic one you just pulled out from your job search portfolio.

To grab the attention of the recruiter, it is essential that you seize the introduction as an avenue to communicate your skills that are relevant to the job and how you have used such skills to achieve professional distinction in the past. Powerfully seize the recruiter's attention with the introduction and you are halfway to successfully utilizing the cover letter.

A Carefully Structured Body

If you were able to seize the attention of the recruiter with your introduction, you must not relent yet. You must now craft your sales pitch in the body of the letter. The body of your cover letter must not exceed two paragraphs. Each of the paragraphs must expatiate on the following details:

- The first paragraph must tell the recruiter why you are "**The One**". Your goal in this paragraph is to show the recruiter how your skill sets would be perfect for the job. Demonstrate with relevant anecdotes how you would use your skills to benefit the company.

- In the second paragraph of the body of the letter, you must communicate reasons you feel the company and position is a perfect fit for you. Here, you must state the way you believe the company's goals are seamlessly aligned to your own career goals. Take the time to enthusiastically state how you believe the company will positively influence your career. A little flattery is not completely uncalled for here.

Closing Paragraph

The closing paragraph is an equally important element of a cover letter. You must write a strong closing paragraph with a compelling call to action. Remember that the cover letter is a letter you use to effectively market yourself. The closing paragraph is where you seal the deal. Do it skillfully!

Complimentary Close

The complimentary close or closing sentiment is how you decisively conclude the letter. It takes the form of "*Sincerely*" followed by your full name. An example of a complimentary close for a cover letter is:

> *Sincerely,*
> *Ben Shawn*

Postscript

Copywriting experts have recorded that a postscript contained in any copy aggressively demands attention. Including a postscript in your cover letter will increase the chances of getting your message across to the recruiter. A postscript stating your willingness to go over any details in your resume or cover letter in a face to face interview is a great way to draw the attention of the recruiter.

These are the nine major elements of a great cover letter that you must always include in your cover letter for maximum efficiency of the letter. Never omit them. However it is important that you realize the fact that the first three items on this list would not be required in your cover letter if you are submitting through a job portal that already has your resume and other relevant details simultaneously submitted on it.

In a nutshell, the elements of a cover letter can be summarized into the three following parts:

1. **Start Strong:** A captivating beginning is an essential element of a cover letter. Strive to begin your cover letter in a manner that would get the recruiter to read further.

2. **Show that You and the Company are Soul mates:** The body of the cover letter must explicitly convey

the ways in which you are the perfect fit for a particular position in the company and how the company is also a perfect fit for you.

3. **Go out in a Blaze of Glory:** Finish your cover letter in a strong and compelling tone. A compelling finish is as important as a captivating beginning. Keep that in mind.

Now that you have the practical knowledge of the elements of a great cover letter. Always implement them whenever you are writing your own cover letter and your letter will stand out in a unique and positive light. Now, we must consider the format of a cover letter.

FORMAT OF A COVER LETTER

A cover letter does not have a specific paper format but it is recommended that you use the following modalities to format your cover letters for optimal efficiency:

- Use only font types like Calibri, Arial, Times New Roman, Georgia and Verdana. Ensure that whichever font type you use in your resume is the same one you use in your cover letter. Consistency is key.

- Use a font size of 12 points. It guarantees maximum clarity without extensively lengthening the cover letter.
- Use a standard margin of 1inch on the left, right, top and bottom margin.

In this chapter, you have learned the major elements of a cover letter and how to appropriately format your cover letter for optimal efficiency with explicit examples of font types and font size to use for your cover letter. Ensure you conform to the instructions and recommendations in this chapter and you'd have created an edge for yourself.

CHAPTER 4

HORRIBLE MISTAKES TO AVOID IN YOUR COVER LETTER

Writing a cover letter riddled with mistakes is the best way to lose a job. If you cannot write a cover letter that is free from basic errors, the recruiter would assume that you are not fit for the company. Outside of the common grammatical mistakes you should be wary of, there are some other mistakes that job applicants make in their cover letter that could jeopardize their chances of getting a job. This chapter will reveal some of these mistakes so that you will never be a victim. Pay special attention to them and immediately correct any of the mistakes you have been making.

MISTAKES TO AVOID IN YOUR COVER LETTER

Mistake 1: Grammar and Spelling Errors

A cover letter is a representation of your communication skills. If you write a cover letter that is so full of grammatical errors, then you will be literally speaking ill of yourself. Spelling errors in a cover letter simply shows you are plain lazy. Always edit your cover letter for grammatical errors, get help if necessary. Use a dictionary to check for spelling errors. Grammatical and spelling errors make the flow of your letter stilted and impossible to read. You can rest assured that it would not be read. Proficiency in communication is an essential part of any job and a cover letter is the first way recruiters assess a candidate's communication proficiency. Strive to leave an excellent first impression.

Mistake 2: Writing in Text Style

Closely related to outright grammatical and spelling errors in writing a cover letter is the use of abbreviations and languages that should be exclusive to texting. No recruiter would read a cover letter with statements written like this: *"I ws d leading insurance agt 4 XYZ company."*Be careful to avoid writing a cover letter in such style. It is repulsive. And you can rest assured that any letter written in such manner will end up in the trash can.

Mistake 3: Using an Unprofessional Email Address

Whether you are submitting your cover letter through an email message or you are simply including your email address in a hard copy of the cover letter you intend to submit physically, never make the mistake of using an unprofessional or personal email address. You will never be taken serious if your email address is something like *ZombieSlayer@abc.com* or *Nathan12345@xyz.com*. Use professional email address for every job you apply for. It may seem insignificant but it is not. Professional email address templates look like the following:

- FirstNameLastName@xyz.com.

  E.g.*BenShawn@xyz.com*

- FirstName.LastName@xyz.com.

  E.g.*Ben.Shawn@xyz.com*

- FirstNameInitialLastName@xyz.com.

  E.g.*BShawn@xyz.com*

- FirstNameLastNameInitial@xyz.com. E.g.

  BenS@xyz.com

Find an available pattern of a professional email address and use it for all your job applications. A professional email address conveys the message that you mean business.

Mistake 4: Using a Generic Cover Letter for All Your Applications

Using an uncustomized, generic letter to apply for jobs in different companies is a sign of laziness. The recruiter will always find out if you use a generic letter or not. Using a generic cover letter that is not specifically customized for the company and position you are applying for reflects negatively on your work ethics and the level of your seriousness about getting the job. Avoid this pitfall. Always write a unique cover letter for each job application that shows the name of the company and the position you are trying to get in that company.

Mistake 5: A Lengthy Cover Letter

The recruiter is likely to have a ton of cover letters and resumes to review and she is unlikely to spend a huge chunk of her time going through one lengthy one. Never submit a long cover letter. It is inconsiderate and detrimental to the recruiter and yourself. A long cover is most likely to go unread and you would have jeopardized your chances of selling yourself.

Mistake 6: Ignoring Specific Requests for Information

In some job adverts, the company requests for candidates that "have specific knowledge of XYZ field", "can use ABC software" or "know how to do _". Many job applicants make the mistake of ignoring these specific requests for information in their cover letters with the assumption that their resumes might convey such information. Others simply ignore it. A horrible mistake! Always use relevant anecdotes to answer such requests for information.

Providing relevant answers to this requests show that you pay attention to details and can follow simple instructions.

Mistake 7: Focusing Only on Your Technical Skills and Ignoring Your Soft Skills

Don't get me wrong, your technical skills are very important in any job application. But your soft skills and ability to deal intelligently with people and situations are equally important. Recruiters want to hire people that are not only competent but also emotionally intelligent. Failure to also communicate your soft skills while overemphasizing your technical skills is a grave mistake. A lot of other applicants also possess the technical skills you do but your soft skills can help you stand out. Always communicate your soft skills in your cover letter. It can yield astonishing results.

Mistake 8: Focusing on Features

Another mistake made by job applicants in their cover letters is to start detailing the qualifications they possess. They erroneously believe that all of the glorious features they possess would be more than sufficient to convince the hiring manager that they are the perfect fit for the company. Realize now that features/qualifications are not enough. You must demonstrate how you can use your qualifications to benefit the organization. Show the hiring manager that you don't just come with big guns but that you can also use them.

Mistake 9: Embellishing Your Accomplishments

While trying to demonstrate their qualifications, some applicants resort to exaggerating and embellishing their accomplishments. That is DISHONESTY. And it may eventually come back to haunt you. In the event that the hiring manager was so impressed with some of your accomplishments and decided to confirm these accomplishments and they turn out to be false, your application will be instantly void and you will be blacklisted. Resist the temptation to be dishonest in your cover letter.

Mistake 10: Portraying Your Current/Previous Employer in a Negative Light

It makes no difference how badly you feel you are being treated by your current employer. Neither does it matter how your previous employer tool advantage of you. The hiring manager does not need to know that you have had experiences with "horrible" employers. Neither does dragging your previous/current employers in the mud help you climb the stairs into a new company. Never write things in your cover letter that speak negatively of your previous or current employers whether they are true or not.

Mistake 11: Non-specific Salutations

Most of us were indoctrinated into the idea that all formal letters must be strictly formal. This may be the ideal way to write a formal letter but you must learn the differences between formality and cold standoffishness. One horrible mistake any applicant can make is to use a seemingly nonchalant greeting to open a cover letter. Salutations like that tell the recruiter that you do not care enough to do proper research that will help you find the name of the person to address your letter to.

Avoid salutations like "Dear Sir/Ma" and "To whom it may concern" at all costs. The former smacks of laziness and nonchalance while the latter is simply off-putting and insulting. Get the name of the right person to address your letter to. It creates a good impression of the candidate when he/she addresses the recruiter by name.

Mistake 12: A Bland Beginning

It's a terrible mistake to begin your cover letter with bland statements like *"I am writing to apply for..."*Your cover letter should instantaneously grab the recruiter's attention, lure them in and get them to read to the end. The beginning of your cover letter is one of the most important parts of the cover letter, don't joke with it. Marketers use a technique termed AIDA to do this kind of thing. AIDA is an acronym for Attention, Interest, Desire and Action. Learn to adopt this technique for writing your cover letters.

Mistake 13: Just Dropping a Laundry List of Your Skills

"I am skilled at x, y and z" or *"I can do 1, 2 and 3"* is a horrible way to introduce your skills in a cover letter. Those things are already covered in the resume. Besides, the recruiter expects you to have such skills. Same as other candidates, so you are not going to impress anyone with a laundry list of what you can do. Rather provide anecdotes that show how you uniquely used those skills to provide value to your previous or current employers. That is what differentiates you and brings out the "wow factor" in your cover letter.

Mistake 14: Giving Excuses for Any Potential Shortfall in Your Resume

If there is any skill or certification that you ought to have acquired at that particular point in time and you are yet to get such skill or certification, the worst thing you could do is to provide "reasonable" excuses as to why you were unable to get such skill or certification. Already dripping with excuses before you have your foot in the door sends a negative message about you to the recruiter. Resist the temptation to provide excuses for shortfalls in your resume.

Mistake 15: Including Your Salary Expectations in a Cover Letter

Here's the thing: no one cares about what you want. Least of all someone you haven't even started working for. Keep your salary expectations to yourself. Never waste the precious few statements you have in a cover letter to lobby for a certain amount of salary. Rather focus on the amazing value you can bring to the company.

In this chapter, you have learned some of the mistakes that jeopardize the effectiveness of a cover letter. Commit them to memory and scrutinize every letter you write to make sure none of these mistakes appear in it. Taking care to avoid these mistakes will help you edge out other applicants who are likely to have their cover letters riddled with these mistakes. More importantly, the recruiter will read your cover letter to the end. And trust me, that can make a world of difference.

In the next couple of chapters, you will learn the secrets to writing a powerful resume that has been helping thousands of people land their dream jobs. Keep reading.

CHAPTER 5

FUNCTIONS AND ELEMENTS OF A RESUME

Now that you have an understanding of what the cover letter is all about, it's now important to learn the mechanics of a captivating resume. You must understand that a great resume is a crucial part of your job applications, and in fact indispensable to getting the job. A fantastic cover letter written in line with the guidelines you've learn within the pages of this book is like foreplay, your resume is the real deal.

It's time you get acquainted with the various details that make a resume stand out and how you can get to implement these details in your own copies of resume.

Functions of a Resume

The first step to actually creating a resume that has the distinction to captivate recruiters' attention and take you one more step ahead of other applicants is for you to understand the true purposes of a resume. It's easy to misconstrue it as simply a piece of paper that does nothing but bombard recruiters with gut-wrenching amount of data. A resume does much more than that. A resume's functions include the following:

1. Showcases your communication skills

At the basic level, a resume demonstrates your ability to communicate effectively. From perusing your resume, a recruiter can determine your ability to organize data, present them coherently and successfully pass information to an observer. He can also gauge your attention to details and overall writing proficiency from the pages of your resume. Typographical and grammatical errors in a resume do not speak highly of your communication skills. It's essential you proofread your resume before sending it. If possible, have a second set of eyes go through it.

2. Introduces you

Recall that your cover letter is supposed to do a kick-ass job of showing recruiters the benefits you can bring to their business. It's expected to be centered almost exclusively on the organization you are applying for. It's within the pages of your resume you get the opportunity to actually introduce yourself to the recruiter. You get the opportunity to toot your own horn. A resume allows you to tell the recruiter your greatest assets.

3. Provides an overview of your career

You get the opportunity to share your own unique "Hero's Journey" within the pages of your resume, in a concise and clear write up. A resume highlights your academic and work experiences. A resume showcases your past responsibilities and achievements at a glance. This is one of the core purposes of a resume. And how you utilize the resume to achieve this has the potential to get you one step closer to the door or leave you wandering beneath a pile of old papers to be recycled.

4. Self positioning

A frequently overlooked function of the resume is the fact that it has the potential to help you brand yourself and produce a specific kind of perception in the minds of recruiters. If you take the opportunity provided by a resume to skillfully calibrate the overview of your career into a specific pattern, you can easily influence the perceptions of recruiters. By highlighting your knowledge, skills, expertise and accomplishments in a specifically tailored manner, you can create an image of yourself as a specific kind of professional and show recruiters that you are not only the real deal, but also the "The One" for their company.

5. Secure an interview

It's the most popular function of a resume. All your preparations during a job application process are targeted at getting a job. But you also realize the fact that securing an interview with the company of your choice is a gigantic leap in the right direction - getting that job. A great resume does an amazing job of getting you that interview. Your resume is like bait. If you put the right kind of bait before the right kind of fish, it'll bite. A fabulous resume seduces recruiters and induces them to call you for an interview. It's the chief aim of a resume.

With that understanding of the various purposes of a resume, you must now endeavor to keep all these purposes in mind whenever you are writing a resume. It's imperative you ensure that every resume you write ticks all the right boxes.

Elements of a Resume

The elements of a resume are the various aspects of a resume. They are the contents that are expected to be displayed in your resume. It's what makes a resume worthy of being called a resume. Every single resume you write must have these elements. The elements of a resume include the following:

- Contact information.

- Resume summary/Resume objective.

- Professional experience.

- Certifications and Licenses.

- Education.

- Skills.

Contact Information

Your contact information is a prominent part of your resume. The contact information section of your resume shows your full name, job title you're applying for, professional email address, phone number, social media profile (especially LinkedIn) and websites if you have any. Bear in mind that it's not a requirement for you to include your physical home address in your resume. But you may do so at your own discretion.

Resume Summary or Resume Objective

Resume summary is quite different from the resume objective. A resume summary is a few lines of words that summarize your entire professional career at a glance.

Here, you are expected to give accounts of various jobs you've held in the past along with the number of years you held the jobs. Your achievements at the jobs should also be recorded here. In short, the three major parts of a resume summary are:

1. Jobs and years of experience.
2. Relevant achievements.
3. Your short term goals.

A typical resume summary would look like:

> *Practicing web developer with 5+ years experience in designing e-commerce websites with integrated payment gateways. Increased sales by 23% after introducing a two-step checkout system. Looking to leverage my web design skills for the position of chief web developer at XYZ Company.*

Bear in mind that only professionals with relevant experience use the resume summary. If you are a fresh graduate, undergoing a major career change or a student looking to land that first internship; you can only use the **resume objective**.

 The resume objective, like the resume summary, is also a very short write up that speaks about your motivations for applying for a specific position rather than the experiences you have that relate to the job.

Understand this: You only use a resume summary in your resume if you possess relevant experiences that could be useful in the job you are currently applying for. And if you're a professional who has been practicing for a couple of years, it's expected that you would have some relevant experiences. But if you're still a fresh graduate, stick to the resume objective. Same applies for those undergoing a career change.

Professional Experience

The professional experience segment of your resume is like a bill board that is exclusively yours to use. Like any bill board, you can use it to aggressively advertise yourself. It's a core component of your resume and you must take care to make it perfect. This segment documents all the relevant job titles you've held in the past, presented in a reverse-chronological order. The implication of this is that the most recent job you've held would appear first.

Components of the experience segment of a resume include:

- Job title.
- Dates you worked in that position.
- Name of company.
- Location of the company.
- 4 to 6 bullet points detailing the core duties you performed for the company.
- Quantifiable results achieved in that position.

It's important that you accompany the duties and responsibilities under "Experience" with results that are backed by numbers. It shows that you have what it takes to generate results when a responsibility is foisted upon you.

Following the above points closely would yield a final result that looks like this:

> ***Creative Director*** *(August 2013 - Present)*
>
> *Curveball Advertising Agency, Austin, TX*
>
> - *Lead a team of 13 professional copywriters.*
> - *Develop marketing strategies for clients resulting in 37% increase in sales.*
> - *Cut marketing costs for clients up to 48% by developing innovative means of reaching the client's target audience.*
> - *Create digital marketing campaigns increasing company's patronage by 27% in 30 days.*

You can also add volunteer experiences that are relevant to the job under this segment. Stick to experiences that are relevant to the position you are applying for. You do not need to provide a record of all the jobs you've held and the responsibilities accompanying those positions. Only the relevant and impressive ones. Remember that the jobs you've held should be recorded in a reverse-chronological order.

Certifications and Licenses

This is not an element of a resume that is universal to all professions. It's only useful to applicants who are involved in a highly professional industry that requires strict certifications and/or licenses. All your relevant certifications should be presented under this segment in the following format:

- Name of certification.
- Name of certifying body/agency.
- Date certified.
- Location (if it's relevant).

Resist the temptation to write your certifications in abbreviated forms. Even if the job posts states the relevant certifications in acronyms, ensure you write out the full name of the certification at least once.

Education

Education is another significant element of a resume. It's especially important for fresh graduates to pay special attention to this segment. Your highest education must come first, and then the rest will follow in a reverse-chronological order. The objective of this arrangement is to put your best qualification ahead of every other while ensuring that the most recent education you've acquired are also given prominence.

The goal of this element is to showcase your academic career and its resulting qualifications. Note the fact that it is bad practice to include your high school information under "Education" if you have a college degree. Resist the urge to mention your GPA if it's anything below 3.5. Anything less than that is not impressive enough to give you an added advantage if it's mentioned in your resume. Information under education should be presented in the following format:

- Type of degree.
- Major.

- Name of School.

- Location of school.

- Year of graduation or anticipated year of graduation.

Here's what an appropriately presented item under the education segment looks like:

Msc in Business Administration

Harvard University, Cambridge, MA

Graduated in   2015 with 3.95 GPA

Skills

Here you list a set of skills that are relevant to the position you are applying for. You must bear in mind that the recruiter expects to see a list of the skills demanded in the job post under this section. So you must pay special attention to every skill mentioned in the job post and make sure you have them all listed in your resume. If you do not have all the required skills listed in a job post, list the ones you have.

It goes without saying that your skills must complement your work experience. If your resume says you have web design skills, it's ideal that you also have experience as a website designer. Otherwise the overall integrity of your resume might be questioned.

While writing your skills under this section, ensure you provide room for both Hard and Soft skills. Hard skills are the technical skills that ensure you can do the job competently, Soft skills on the other hand are those non-technical skills you possess that show recruiters that you can get the job done smoothly. Leadership skills, communication skills and teamwork are example of soft skills that are useful to add to your resume.

Avoid providing a laundry list of all your skills, rather use short and concise sentences to present your skills. Here are some examples of how to present your skills:

- Proficient in graphics design packages, including Photoshop and CorelDraw.

- Able to create high quality animated videos.

- Excellent communication skills.

- Etc.

Realize that the elements of a resume covered in this section are the core elements of every resume. However it's not uncommon to have a variation of the elements of a resume. Some people are wont to include other sections like hobbies and interests, awards and honors, volunteer works, projects, etc in their resumes. But keep in mind that every single thing you include in your resume must work to your advantages if you think any of those add-ons would do you good, add them.

CHAPTER 6

FORMATTING A RESUME CORRECTLY

Studies show that about 75 percent of big organizations use Applicant Tracking System (A.T.S) to review resumes. The end result of this is that about 70 percent of resumes go unread. Resumes that fail to pass the Applicant Tracking System are promptly discarded. The reason most resumes fail to pass the ATS can be linked to horrible formatting of their resume.

When a resume is woefully formatted, it makes it difficult for the ATS robots to read such resumes. Thus, the resume goes unread. In this chapter, you will learn how to format your resume like a professional. And get the resume to pass the Applicant Tracking System and still appeal to human readers.

In this chapter, you will also learn what "Consistency" means in resume writing and how to practice consistency when writing your resume.

Let's get right into it.

FONTS

Fonts are principal aspects of formatting your resume. All the contents in your resume are presented in a flow of fonts. Like individual handwritings, fonts also convey unique messages. So it's advisable you pay special attention to the fonts you use in your resume.

Experts have identified eight perfect fonts for writing a resume that looks professional, and are easy to read by both humans and ATS bots, they include:

1. Times New Roman.
2. Calibri.
3. Arial.
4. Georgia.
5. Garamond.

6. Helvetica.

7. Tahoma.

8. Verdana.

These fonts are the most popular fronts in resume writing and they are ideal for writing your resume. Times New Roman in particular is the most used fonts when it comes to writing resume.

It is important that you stick to a single font when writing your resume. It makes your resume look clean and uniform. If you are ever tempted to use more than one font in your resume, under no circumstances should you use more than two fonts.

 It is also good practice to use the same font for both your cover letter and resume. Light fonts are difficult to read on a computer screen or in print, avoid them.

FONT SIZE

Font size is a key element that makes it possible for your resume to look well organized and presentable. The ideal font size for writing a resume is between 10-12 pts. It makes it possible for you to have an appealing combination of black texts and white spaces.

The only exception to font sizes comes in form of the headings of the various sections of your resumes. Take care to use a single font size for the body of your resume.

FONT STYLE

Font styles can be used to draw attention to specific details in your resume. But they must be used with care and discretion. Ideally, you can use a bold font style for your section headings. Although there's no law against underlining the headlines either but it is less professional. The three kinds of highlights that could be used to differentiate your section headings are:

- Increasing the size of the fonts.
- Using a bold font.

- Underlining it.

Observe that two of the three methods are based on font styles. However, you can increase the font size and use a bold font style at the same time to get optimal results.

Bear in mind that the use of font styles is mostly restricted to section headings and positions held in the past. You must keep the actual body of the resume as simple as possible.

LINE SPACING

The spacing for your resume should also be taken as an important element of professional resume presentation. The ideal line spacing for a resume is a single spacing. If you want more spacing, then go for a 1.15 line spacing. You can, however, increase the spacing if you are just starting to build your resume. But always keep the spacing below 1.5.

Keep in mind that when you are writing a section heading in your resume, you must leave a space before and after every single one of the headings.

MARGINS

The margins in your resume can have significant influence in the eventual layout of the resume. It should be chosen with great care. A margin of one (1) inch should be used for both the left and right margins. A similar measurement, i.e. one inch, should also be used for the top and bottom margins.

Now that you have a comprehensive idea of how to format a resume, let's consider what consistency means in resume writing.

CONSISTENCY IN RESUME

Consistency is a big deal when you are writing a resume. Consistency in resume writing simply implies that you must follow a single defined pattern of doing things in your resume. Once you adopt a way of doing things in your resume, you must stick to it throughout the entire resume.

It allows your resume to flow in a predictable, easy to follow manner. An inconsistent resume elicits a jarring reaction from readers. Emphasis should be placed on keeping your entire resume consistent.

Here are some core areas to look out for consistency issues in your resume:

- **Dates**: Always stick to a single format when you write dates in your resume. Once you start using a particular format of date, use that format throughout your resume. For instance, if you start with a format like *April 3, 2013,* consistency dictates you use that format for every single date you write in that resume. Using another date format like *3-04-2013* is a horrible consistency flop.

- **Fonts**: Switching between different kinds of font within a single resume document is a great breach of the consistency rule. Reading a document that started with a Times New Roman font, then suddenly have it switched to the Verdana font and back to Times New Roman after a while is not a beautiful experience. A document presented in such a manner is sure to cause a hitch in the reading experience of readers - whether humans or bots. Consistency here means sticking to a single font throughout the resume.

- **Font Size**: A resume must also have a consistent use of font sizes. All sections of the document must be written in the same font size. It makes no sense to write the professional experience section with size 10 fonts and then switch to size 12 in the skills section. The only effect that would achieve is to showcase how unorganized you are with your resume.

- **Font Style**: Styling your resume also demands consistency. If you decide to use a bold font style for the section heading, do so for every single section heading in the resume. Don't use a bold font style for some headings and then underline others within the same document. That is not acceptable practice.

Overall your resume must be expertly formatted if you will get the best results with it. With the resume formatting guidelines provided in this chapter, you can now correctly format your resume. You now understand the best formatting practices for a resume, take care to deploy them whenever you are writing a resume. The subject of consistency in resume writing has also been copiously explained and the importance emphasized. Keep the lessons in this chapter in mind whenever you write a resume for yourself or for someone else and you'd have given the owner of the resume a competitive advantage over other applicants.

CHAPTER 7

MISTAKES TO AVOID IN WRITING A RESUME

When you are writing a resume, there are certain mistakes that could completely ruin the resume and render it useless. Some of these mistakes are simply annoying while others move beyond pesky to outright horrible.

Knowing the kinds of mistakes that could jeopardize the efficacy of your resume would help you avoid them and create a resume that is "healthy" and ready.

In this chapter, you'll learn some of the mistakes that plague job applicants when it comes to writing a resume. The aim of this chapter is to help you avoid every single one of these mistakes so that you can triple your chances of getting the job you want.

Here are some of the mistakes you must avoid at all costs when you write a resume:

Mistake 1: Spelling and Grammatical Errors

It may seem redundant that this is on the list but you'll be shocked at the amount of resumes riddled with typographical and grammatical errors. A resume with grammatical or typographical errors brings your communication skills into question. Typographical errors are especially bad. They show that you do not care enough about the job to proofread and correct simple spelling mistakes. Avoid this type of mistakes in your resume at all costs.

Mistake 2: Using an Unprofessional Email Address

Your email address should look professional. Using a silly email address is a silly mistake. Stick to professional emails that incorporate your full names or a variation of it.

Mistake 3: Incorrect Contact Details

This is a great disadvantage to yourself rather than a negative representation of your resume. Imagine impressing a recruiter with all the skills and accomplishments in your resume and they try to call you for an interview just to find out that you'd written a wrong number in your contact details. Double check your contact details and make sure they are correct before sending out your resume.

Mistake 4: Including Personal Details

Personal details like your age, marital status, personal hobbies, home address, etc are irrelevant on your resume. Your employer and colleagues will get to know all those details when you start working at the organization. But first, get in. Including irrelevant details like these in your resume could actually ruin your chances of getting in.

 The only time you could take the liberty of including your personal hobby in your resume is if your prior research about the company shows a company culture, objective or values that aligns with said hobby. For instance if you love volunteering at the local clinic three days a month and your research shows the company is strongly committed to social responsibilities, you could include such a hobby in your resume. Otherwise, keep your resume free of personal details.

Mistake 5: Including a Photo of Yourself

Most official documents require a headshot photograph to accompany them, so the temptation to include same in your resume is understandable. But never give in. You do not need to include a photograph in your resume unless it is specifically demanded by the job post.

Mistake 6: Using a Single Resume for Various Job Applications

This is a terrible practice that can hamper your chances of successfully getting a job. A one-size-fits-all resume will be too generic and recruiters will pick up on that and conclude that you have no special interest in their company. That you're just looking for 'any' job. Even if that's the case, you don't want to make it obvious. Endeavor to customize your resume to fit an individual company and job posts. This will tell recruiters that you are especially enthusiastic about working for their company. And that can work in your favor.

Mistake 7: Ignoring Specific Application Instructions

Failing to provide information, details or adhere to specific guidelines while submitting your resume is a grievous mistake that can threaten your chances of getting the job. It shows that you do not pay attention to details. Or that you just don't care what the hiring manager wants because you are too fixated on what you want. Either way, you can say goodbye to the job. So it's advisable for you to adhere to application instructions.

Mistake 8: Lengthy Resume

Fact is the hiring manager might need to go through as much as 250 resumes for a single job post. Submitting a lengthy resume filled with redundant and irrelevant information would not do you any good. Such a resume will cause the recruiter to feel overwhelmed and they might simply discard your resume, along with your chances of getting a job, without reading it. If they are considerate enough to read it, they might not get to the best parts before feeling overwhelmed. Again, the resume will be discarded. It's important you keep your resume concise and compact.

Mistake 9: Too Brief Resume

Some applicants in a bid to avoid mistake 8, end up with a resume that is too short. They end up compressing the entire resume into a single page void of any of their tangible achievements. A resume that is too short is likely to be missing vital information that could have increased your chances of getting the job. Strive to create a balanced resume and avoid leaving out important details in a bid to create a short resume.

Mistake 10: Using Dense Blocks of Texts

A block of text that goes on and on, with seemingly no end to it, can be very scary. And not only because of how tasking reading it would be, but scary because it can actually ruin your chances of achieving the aim of your resume. Large blocks of texts in your resume, or anywhere really, can get readers feeling overwhelmed before they even begin to read it. Break down your texts into short blocks of texts and summarize the contents of your resume to provide a short but concise material for the recruiter.

Mistake 11: Using Too Many Bullet Points

Just like mistake 10, too many bullet points in a resume will leave the recruiter feeling overwhelmed. Stick to a maximum of six bullet points to convey cogent information so that the recruiter can be encouraged to read them. Too many bullet points will lead to a case of "Too Long; Didn't Read" and that's bad news for you.

Mistake 12: Using an Objective Statement

As a professional with a rich professional experience, it's a horrible mistake to use a resume objective in your resume. Instead use a professional resume summary to highlight your rich experiences.

Mistake 13: A Bad Resume Summary

Another grave mistake that professionals make in their resume is offering a terrible summary of their professional career in the resume. Using generic statements that does not focus on specific values that you offered in the past, and can offer to the new organization is a minus to your resume.

Mistake 14: Focusing on Duties Instead of Accomplishments

Highlighting only your responsibilities in a former position without stating the accomplishments in that position does not reflect well on you. You must never fail to provide quantifiable results achieved in the positions you occupied in the past. Specific results expressed in terms of numbers will show recruiters your true impact in the organizations you worked for in the past. And those quantitative statistics can help you to reel them in even further. Never make the mistake of omitting them.

Mistake 15: Excessive Use of Buzzwords

Fluffy language aimed at impressing recruiters does one thing and one thing only - the exact opposite. Avoid them. You don't need to tell recruiters how "awesome", "experienced" and "accomplished" you are. The numbers will speak for themselves, and for you. And numbers don't lie. Buzz words are simply repulsive to recruiters. They are like smokescreens intended to mislead. Never use them.

Mistake 16: Keyword Stuffing

Some applicants tend to stuff their resumes with keywords in a bid to pass the Applicant Tracking System (ATS). This is a huge mistake on their part. After passing the ATS, the recruiter gets to review the resume. He's going to discover what you did and the result isn't going to be pretty. Some applicants even have an entire section in their resume dedicated to keywords. Don't be one of those applicants. Use keywords naturally and judiciously in your resume and you would be all right.

These are some of the major mistakes that could ruin a resume and jeopardize your chances of getting the job you want. Keep them in mind whenever you are writing a resume and ensure you avoid them. A resume devoid of these mistakes would be a great advantage to you. Make that advantage yours by avoiding these mistakes.